The Supermom Detox:

Reclaiming Your Time, Sanity and Self

Jessica Belch

1

The Supermom Detox:

Reclaiming Your Time, Sanity and Self

For my Mémé Pelletier,

The queen Super (Grand) Mom who would cut the crusts off my grilled cheese before cooking it, creating the perfect balance of crispy and cheesy. A quiet lesson that love lives in the details — warm, steady, and just right.

She made ployes like she was born for it: never flipping them, letting the tiny holes form perfectly so they could soak up the butter and sit beside her famous chicken stew.

She pulled me safely under the covers when bats got loose during sleepovers (okay, it was just once, but a memory to last a lifetime), and her home always smelled like lilacs in the summer.

She showed me that care doesn't have to be loud to be powerful — it just has to be constant.

Part 1: Why You Can't Breathe

Part 2: Making Space in Your Mind

Part 3: Making Space in Your Life

Part 4: Living With Space

Introduction

For the Mom Who Feels Like She's Lost Herself

You smile.

You show up.

You get through the days.

From the outside, it might look like you're doing "fine."

But inside, something feels quieter than it used to. Heavier. Like pieces of you have slowly gone missing somewhere between diapers, deadlines, dinner plans, emotional labor, and the constant pull of needing to be everything for everyone.

If you've ever wondered, *When did I become this tired version of myself?* — this book is for you.

This isn't the kind of exhaustion that a good night's sleep fixes.

It's the exhaustion of carrying too much for too long.

The kind that settles into your body and convinces you that this is just what motherhood feels like now.

But it doesn't have to be.

The Moment That Changed Everything

One day, completely out of the blue, my ten-year-old looked at me and said:

> *"You smile an awful lot… but I can tell you're actually really sad inside."*

There was no accusation in his voice. No judgment. Just observation.

And it stopped me cold.

Because he was right.

I had been smiling through burnout.
Pushing through exhaustion.
Convincing myself that if I could just be more
grateful, more disciplined, more "together," things
would eventually feel better.

I had tried different tactics before — self-help
strategies, mindset shifts, promises to do better
"next time." But they were always met with
resistance from the world around me, and I folded
quickly because I didn't see the urgency.

I thought I was hiding it well.

I didn't know *he* could see it.

And once I realized he did, something shifted. I
knew I couldn't keep living that way — not because
I needed to be happier for appearances, but because
I didn't want him growing up believing that
burnout, exhaustion, never asking for help, and

quietly accepting misery was what a good life looked like.

I didn't want that to be the model I handed him.

When Survival Mode Becomes a Way of Life

So many moms are surviving — not because they're weak, but because they've been strong for too long.

We learn early how to push through.
How to minimize our needs.
How to be the dependable one.

And for moms with trauma histories, this often goes even deeper. Survival mode once kept you safe. It helped you adapt, cope, and endure. But what protects you in one season can quietly suffocate you in another.

Eventually, surviving stops being enough.

Not because you're ungrateful.

Not because you're failing.

But because your nervous system, your body, and your heart are asking for something more sustainable.

What I Saw Again and Again

Through my counseling practicum and internship, I worked with mothers who were consistently putting their own needs on the back burner. Different backgrounds. Different stories. Different struggles.

But one thing was always the same.

None of them were lazy, broken, or lacking motivation.

They were deeply exhausted.
Profoundly disconnected from themselves.
And quietly carrying the belief that their needs mattered less than everyone else's.

They loved their children fiercely.

They showed up every day.

And they were running on empty.

Many had tried traditional self-care advice and felt
like failures when it didn't stick. What they needed
wasn't another checklist — they needed safety,
permission, and compassion.

This Is Why I Wrote This Book

I wrote this book because I believe motherhood
should not require the slow erasure of yourself.

I believe moms don't need to be told to "try
harder," "stay positive," or "just make time."

I believe healing happens when we stop asking,
What's wrong with me? and start asking, *What
happened to me — and what do I need now?*

This book was written for the mom who:

- Feels like she's lost herself somewhere along the way

- Is tired of surviving but unsure how to thrive

- Loves her family deeply and still wants more than exhaustion

- Wants to feel like herself again — or maybe meet herself for the first time

What This Book Is (and What It Is Not)

This book is not about becoming a perfect mom. It's not about rigid routines, toxic positivity, or fixing yourself.

You are not broken.

This *is* a trauma-informed guide to gently coming back to yourself.
It's about nervous system safety, boundaries, rest,

self-compassion, and redefining what a "good life" actually looks like — for *you*.

You won't find shame here.
You won't find pressure to change everything at once.
You will find permission to slow down, reflect, and choose differently.

How to Use This Book

There is no "right" way to move through these pages.

You can read cover to cover.
You can skip around.
You can pause when something feels tender.

If a chapter stirs something up, it's okay to take a break. If you skip a week — or a month — you haven't failed. Healing is not linear, and growth does not require urgency.

Let this book meet you where you are.

An Invitation

This is an invitation — not an expectation.

An invitation to stop abandoning yourself.
To release the belief that suffering is required.
To show your children what it looks like to live a
life that includes rest, joy, boundaries, and
authenticity.

You don't have to rush.
You don't have to get it right.

You just have to be willing to begin.

And you already have.

Part 1:

Why You Can't Breathe

Chapter 1

The Invisible Load of Motherhood —

Why you're exhausted before the day even starts.

The Day I Realized I Was Holding My Breath

I didn't notice I was holding my breath until my nine-year-old asked me why my face looked "mad" while I was buttering his toast.

It wasn't that I was mad. I was just… tense. Shoulders up, jaw clenched, lungs tight, running through the day's mental checklist before I'd even had my coffee. What a nightmare. There were papers to write. Presentations to prepare. Emails to answer. The laundry that had been sitting on my seat on the couch for two days (which honestly just proved how little I'd actually rested — if I hadn't even needed my spot on the couch). Graduation was coming up, and I still hadn't put in my application. My own needs? Somewhere at the bottom of the list, right below "locate his left shoe" and "remember to feed the dog."

What struck me later wasn't just how long the list was — it was how *automatic* it felt. I wasn't consciously choosing to ignore myself. I didn't wake up thinking, *Today I'll run myself into the ground.* It just happened, quietly and consistently, one small sacrifice at a time.

And here's the thing — I wasn't even having a bad day. This was my normal. It was just the way life was, and I never really questioned it.

For years, I believed that relief was something I had to earn. If I just worked harder, organized better, woke up earlier, or stayed up later, eventually I'd reach some magical point where everything felt manageable. Instead, I kept running faster on a treadmill that never stopped. It was only a matter of time before I tripped... and we've all seen those gym Instagram reels. Yikes.

I wore "busy" like a badge of honor because that's what good moms do... right? They give everything for their family. They sacrifice. They push through. They smile even when they're depleted. No second thought. No complaints.

Somewhere along the way, I stopped checking in with myself altogether. I stopped noticing how my body felt. I stopped asking what I needed. I stopped breathing deeply — literally and figuratively.

Until one day, it hit me: I wasn't actually living. I was surviving... and barely.

That moment wasn't dramatic. There was no breakdown or life-altering event. Just a piece of toast, a curious kid, and the realization that my body had been bracing for impact all day, every day, as if something terrible was always about to happen.

If you're reading this, maybe you've had a moment like that too — the quiet realization that you've been running on fumes for so long, you can't remember what it feels like to just *be*. To breathe without rushing. To exist without performing.

This book is for you.

It's not another "be more productive" manual or a "just practice self-care" pep talk. You don't need another checklist. You don't need a better planner or a prettier morning routine. You don't need more to do — you need *less*.

Less pressure.
Less guilt.
Less noise in your mind.

What you need is space — space to think, to feel, to rest, to exist without constantly managing everything and everyone around you.

Over the next chapters, we're going to talk about why that space feels so hard to find, what's been stealing it from you, and — most importantly — how to get it back *without blowing up your whole life*. You'll get tools you can use right away, not someday. And yes, you'll still be able to keep your kids alive, your boss reasonably satisfied, and your house mostly standing in the process (I'm good, but I'm not a miracle worker).

We'll start where I started: with one deep breath, and a decision to stop running — just for a moment.

The Invisible Load of Motherhood

Here's what they don't tell you about motherhood: it's not just about the physical work.

Yes, there are meals to cook, floors to clean, and tiny socks to match — but that's only the visible layer. That's the part people notice, praise, and sometimes even help with.

Underneath is the invisible load — the mental and emotional labor that never gets clocked out of. The work that lives in your head. The work that follows you into the shower, into bed, and into your dreams.

It's remembering your child's shoe size without checking.
It's tracking when permission slips are due.
It's knowing which kid hates crusts this week.
It's noticing your partner seems stressed and wondering whether to say something or give them space.
It's the 2 a.m. math of, *If I fall asleep right now, I'll get four hours and seventeen minutes.*

And the thing about the invisible load is that no one hands it to you — you just pick it up, piece by piece, until one day you realize you're carrying everything.

No one sees you managing the emotional temperature of the house. No one notices the constant prioritizing, anticipating, and adjusting you do to keep everything running smoothly. And because it's invisible, it rarely gets acknowledged.

One morning, I completely lost it over a container of blueberries that slipped out of my hand at breakfast. Full meltdown. Tears streaming. That deep, guttural frustration that feels disproportionate even as it's happening.

But it wasn't about the blueberries.

It was about the thousand other things stacked in my head — the appointments, the deadlines, the emotional needs, the expectations — piled so high that one tiny thing falling off the top sent everything crashing down.

That's how overload works. It's rarely the *big* thing that breaks you. It's the accumulation.

Why We Accept It as Normal

Here's the dangerous part: most of us believe this is just how life is supposed to feel.

We watched women before us do it all — mothers, grandmothers, aunts who ran households, raised children, worked jobs, and kept smiling. We learned early that "good moms put themselves last." That sacrifice equals love. That exhaustion is proof you're doing it right.

And then culture doubled down.

Busy became a status symbol. If your calendar isn't full, if you're not overwhelmed, if you're not exhausted — are you even trying? Somewhere along the way, rest became laziness and boundaries became selfishness.

Add social media to the mix, where everyone else's house looks calm and curated while yours is one missing blue spoon away from total chaos, and it's no wonder we internalize the message that *we* are the problem.

So we tell ourselves:
"This is fine."
"This is normal."
"Everyone feels like this."

But normal doesn't mean healthy.
And it definitely doesn't mean sustainable.

The Cost of Constant Tension

Living in a constant state of tension has a price — and you're paying it whether you realize it or not.

Emotionally, it looks like snapping at your kids over small things. Feeling resentful toward your partner. Crying in the shower because it's the only place no one needs anything from you.

Physically, it shows up as headaches, jaw pain, tight shoulders, shallow breathing, poor sleep. You might get sick more often, or feel like you never fully bounce back, even from something minor.

Mentally, it's decision fatigue, forgetfulness, and that foggy feeling where you walk into a room and can't remember why you're there.

Think of your mind like a web browser with thirty-seven tabs open. Even if you're not actively clicking on each one, they're all draining your energy in the background.

No wonder you're exhausted.

And the hardest part? Most of us don't realize how depleted we are until we're already past empty.

Action Step: Your First Breathing Space

Before we go any further, I want you to try something.

Not tomorrow.

Not when the house is quiet.

Right now.

1. Put both feet on the ground.

2. Drop your shoulders. Unclench your jaw. Let your hands rest in your lap.

3. Close your eyes (finish reading this first;)).

4. Inhale slowly through your nose for four counts.

5. Hold for four counts.

6. Exhale through your mouth for six counts.

7. Repeat five times.

As you breathe, say to yourself: *It's safe to pause.*

Notice how your body feels right now — maybe your chest feels a little looser, maybe your mind feels just a fraction quieter. That's not magic. That's you stepping off the hamster wheel for sixty seconds.

Journal/Reflection Prompt:

"Where in my day do I feel most tense, and what's one small thing I can let go of this week to make space for myself to help relieve some of that tension?"

Closing the Chapter

If you just exhaled for what feels like the first time all week, you're not broken.
You're just human.

And you're not alone.

In the next chapter, we're going to start dismantling the *myth of the supermom* — the lie that's been keeping you from the life you actually want and replacing it with something far more freeing.

Chapter 2

The Myth of the Supermom —

How cultural pressure sets you up to fail.

The Problem with Capes and Crowns

When I was little, I thought my mom was a superhero. To be honest, I still do — but for wildly different reasons now.

She cleaned the house, worked full-time, helped with homework, drove me to basketball practice, dance practice, karate class, and whatever other phase I was in. She brought my gym clothes when I "forgot" them at home. She handled all the chaos, stress, and nonsense we threw at her with what looked like style and grace.

She never asked for help.
She never let on that she was tired.

She always seemed capable, composed, and in control.

At least, that's how it looked from the outside.

What I didn't see then — and what so many of us don't see growing up — is what happens *behind* the cape.

I didn't see the moments she cried because this wasn't the life she had imagined for herself. I didn't see how often she swallowed her own needs, desires, and dreams to keep everyone else comfortable. I didn't see the quiet grief of realizing that taking care of everyone else left very little room to take care of herself.

Those conversations didn't happen until well into my adulthood — and when they did, they hit me like a ton of bricks. The woman I had looked up to for "doing it all" had been paying a steep, invisible price.

Sound familiar?

So many of us inherit this image of the "Supermom" like a family heirloom — polished, admired, and passed down with pride. But what no one tells you is how heavy it is to carry. And without realizing it, we slip the cape over our own shoulders, convinced that this is simply what good mothers do.

We don't question it. We emulate it.

Where the Myth Comes From

The Supermom ideal didn't just appear out of thin air. It was carefully constructed — reinforced over decades — and passed down until it felt like fact.

It comes from three major sources.

Generational Modeling

We watched our mothers and grandmothers do it all because that's what was expected of them. They ran households, raised children, and often worked outside the home — all without complaining, asking for help, or setting boundaries. Not because it was healthy, but because it was *necessary*. There was no language for burnout. No permission for rest. No alternative narrative.

It was survival, dressed up as strength.

Cultural Narratives

Movies, TV shows, and magazines have long romanticized motherhood as something you're supposed to love every second of. Exhaustion gets reframed as "blessed chaos." Struggle becomes something you should be grateful for.

You mention being tired as a first-time mom, and someone chirps, "Enjoy it while it lasts — they don't stay little forever."
Like… damn, Susan. I didn't say I hated my kid. I said I'm exhausted.

So we learn to stop sharing the hard parts. We learn to smile through it. We learn that honesty makes people uncomfortable — and that discomfort is apparently worse than suffering in silence.

Social Media Pressure
And then came social media, which poured gasoline on an already burning fire.

Now we're bombarded with images of Instagram-perfect moms in matching outfits, packing organic lunches, running businesses, maintaining spotless homes, and somehow still looking like they just walked out of a spa.

Here's the truth: most of that is curated crap.

Life isn't that polished. Not all the time. Not for anyone. But when we're scrolling at midnight, already exhausted and questioning ourselves, it *feels* real. And comparison quietly creeps in, convincing us that everyone else is doing motherhood better than we are.

All of this creates a Frankenstein's monster of expectations:

Be nurturing like June Cleaver.
Be ambitious like a Fortune 500 CEO.
Be attractive like your body never carried children.
Be available like you don't have a self outside of motherhood.

No wonder we feel like we're failing. The standard was never human to begin with.

Why It's So Hard to Let Go

Even when we *know* this image isn't real, we keep chasing it. Why?

Because it's no longer just about motherhood — it's about worth.

Somewhere along the way, many of us internalized these beliefs:

"If I can handle it all, I'm valuable."

"If I need help, I'm failing."

"If I rest, I'm lazy."

"If I put myself first, I'm selfish."

So we overfunction.

We overcommit.

We overgive.

We say yes when we mean no. We stretch ourselves thinner and thinner. And when we inevitably hit a wall, we don't question the system — we question *ourselves*.

What's wrong with me?

Why can't I handle this like everyone else?

Why am I so tired?

The problem isn't you.

The problem is the impossible standard you were handed and told to live up to.

The Hidden Damage of the Supermom Myth

Constantly playing the superhero comes with consequences — even if they're subtle at first.

It isolates you. When everyone thinks you "have it together," it feels unsafe to admit when you're struggling. You become the strong one, the capable one — and strength becomes a cage.

It steals your joy. When every moment feels like a performance, you can't fully experience your life. You're always managing, anticipating, fixing — never fully present.

And perhaps most painfully, it passes the burden forward.

Your kids are watching. They learn what love looks like by observing how you treat yourself. When they see you ignoring your own needs, pushing through exhaustion, and sacrificing without limits, they internalize that message.

For me, that realization was the hardest pill to swallow.

The Supermom myth doesn't just hurt you — it shapes the next generation.

Your Permission Slip to Take Off the Cape

You don't have to earn your worth by doing it all. You don't have to prove you're a good mom by running yourself into the ground.

What you actually need isn't more effort — it's more support.

Support without shame.
Rest without guilt.
Boundaries without apology.

Taking off the cape doesn't mean you stop caring. It means you stop abandoning yourself in the process of caring for everyone else.

And that? That's not weakness.

That's the beginning of something much healthier.

Action Step: Your "Not Today" List

Instead of adding more to your plate, I want you to make a **Not Today List**:

1. Write down three things you normally do out of perceived obligation, guilt, or habit.

2. Circle the one that drains you the most.

3. For the next week, consciously *don't* do it.

4. Notice how the world doesn't fall apart — and how you feel a little freer.

Example:

- Baking for every school fundraiser.

- Replying to texts immediately.

- Cleaning the kitchen before bed no matter how tired you are.

Journal/Reflection Prompt:

"If I took off the cape, what would change for me? What might change for my family?"

Closing the Chapter

The Supermom myth is powerful because it's everywhere — in our upbringing, in our culture, in our feeds.
But the truth is, you were never meant to be everything for everyone.

Later in this book (Chapter 4), we'll explore *how to give yourself permission to pause* — and why that single choice could be the most radical act of motherhood you'll ever make.

Chapter 3

Signs You're Running on Empty - From irritability to physical burnout.

The Boiling Frog Problem

You've probably heard the old saying: if you put a frog in boiling water, it'll jump out. But if you put it in cool water and slowly turn up the heat, it won't notice until it's too late.

Burnout works the same way.

Most moms don't wake up one day and think, *Wow, I'm completely depleted.* There's no dramatic moment where a siren goes off announcing that you've officially hit empty.

Instead, we adjust.

We adjust to being a little more tired than yesterday.
A little more irritable.
A little less patient.
A little less joyful.

We normalize it. We tell ourselves this is just what this season looks like. And because motherhood comes in waves — newborns, school years, activities, work demands — there's always a reason to push through.

Until one day, we pause long enough to realize we've been running on fumes for months... or even years.

The problem isn't that the signs weren't there.
 It's that we've been trained to ignore them.

The Everyday Red Flags

Running on empty doesn't always look like collapsing in bed at 2 p.m. or having a dramatic breakdown in the middle of Target (though sometimes it does). More often, it shows up quietly — in ways that feel easy to explain away.

Here are some of the most common signs.

1. You're Always Irritable
The kids spill water and your body reacts like an alarm has gone off. Someone chews too loudly and it feels unbearable. You snap faster than you want to, then feel guilty afterward.

This isn't because you're "angry" or "impatient." It's because your nervous system is overloaded. When your emotional reserves are depleted, even minor stressors feel like major threats.

2. Everything Feels Like "Too Much"
The grocery store feels overwhelming. The thought of making dinner feels like climbing Everest. One more request — even a small one — feels like the final straw.

This is a capacity issue, not a character flaw. When you're running on empty, your system doesn't have room to hold anything extra.

3. You're Forgetting the Basics

You walk into a room and forget why you're there. You lose your phone while holding it. You miss appointments or forget conversations.

This isn't you "losing it." Chronic stress impacts memory and focus. Your brain is prioritizing survival, not recall.

4. You've Stopped Caring About Things You Used to Enjoy

Hobbies feel like work. Date night sounds exhausting. Even watching your favorite show feels like too much effort.

When you're depleted, pleasure shuts down. Your system is conserving energy, not seeking joy.

5. You Feel Tired… Even After Rest

You finally get a full night of sleep — or at least more than usual — and still wake up exhausted.

That's a sign your fatigue goes deeper than physical tiredness. Mental load, emotional labor, and nervous system dysregulation don't reset with sleep alone.

6. Your Body Feels Tight All the Time

Jaw clenched. Shoulders up near your ears. Stomach in knots. You might not even notice it anymore — it just feels like how your body exists.

This is your body stuck in fight-or-flight mode, bracing for the next problem before it even arrives.

7. You Zone Out More Than You'd Like

Scrolling endlessly. Binge-watching. Staring into space. Zoning out isn't laziness — it's a form of self-protection. Your system is desperate for a break, even if the break isn't actually restorative.

The Emotional Signs We Don't Talk About

Beyond the obvious symptoms, running on empty also shows up emotionally.

You feel numb instead of sad or happy.
You feel disconnected from yourself and others.
You feel like you're "going through the motions" of your own life.

You might even start wondering what's wrong with you — why you don't feel more grateful, more patient, more fulfilled.

Nothing is wrong with you.
You're depleted.

Why We Ignore the Signs

Moms are master justifiers.

"It's just a busy season."
"I'll rest once things calm down."

"Other people have it worse."
"This is just part of motherhood."

We minimize our own experience because we've been taught that exhaustion equals dedication. That burnout is the price of being a good mom. That if we admit we're struggling, we're somehow failing.

So we push past the warning signs instead of listening to them.

But here's the truth: constant depletion isn't normal. It's common — but it's not healthy.

The Cost of Running on Empty

If you keep going without refilling your tank, the cost compounds.

You snap at the people you love the most.
You miss small moments of joy because you're too tired to notice them.

You start feeling resentful, disconnected, or emotionally flat.

Physically, your body starts keeping score. Chronic stress contributes to headaches, digestive issues, hormone disruption, weakened immunity, and persistent pain.

Emotionally, you lose access to patience, curiosity, and compassion — not because you don't care, but because there's nothing left to give.

The scariest part?

If you run on empty long enough, empty becomes your baseline. You forget what it feels like to be calm. To feel spacious. To exist without tension humming under the surface.

And that's exactly why noticing the signs matters.

Because awareness isn't weakness — it's the first step toward change.

Action Step: Check Your Tank

Today, take five quiet minutes and rate yourself
from 1–10 on these:

- **Physical energy** (How rested do you feel?)

- **Emotional energy** (How much patience and
  joy do you have?)

- **Mental clarity** (How focused and clear is
  your thinking?)

If you're below a 6 in any category, it's time to
make changes now — before your tank runs dry.

Journal/Reflection Prompt:

"Which of these signs feels most familiar
right now? How is it showing up in my life?"

Closing the Chapter

Recognizing you're running on empty isn't about shaming yourself — it's about catching the warning signs before burnout takes over completely.

In the next chapter, we'll talk about **how to give yourself permission to pause**, and why that choice might be the simplest, most radical way to start refilling your tank.

Part 2:

Making Space in Your Mind

Chapter 4

Permission to Pause - Why slowing down is a power move

The Lie About Stopping

If I asked you, *"When was the last time you took a break in the middle of the day — just because you wanted to?"* - what would you say?

Most moms laugh when I ask that. Not because it's funny, but because the idea feels so unrealistic it borders on absurd. A break in the middle of the day? On purpose? Without earning it first? That feels about as likely as a solo vacation to Paris.

Here's the lie we've been fed:

If you pause, you'll fall behind.
If you slow down, you're lazy.
If you rest, you're not pulling your weight.

So we keep moving.
We keep producing.
We keep "just getting through the day," as if momentum is the only thing holding our lives together.

We treat ourselves like machines — valuable only when we're running, accomplishing, checking things off. And the idea of stopping feels dangerous, like everything might collapse if we do.

But here's the truth no one tells you:

You can't sustain a life you never stop aggressively living.

Pause isn't weakness — it's maintenance.
It's not quitting — it's recalibrating.

It's not giving up — it's choosing to stay in the game long-term.

Why We Don't Give Ourselves Permission

Even when we technically *have* a free moment, it rarely feels free.

We fill it with laundry.
We tidy something real quick.
We scroll on our phones while half-thinking about what still needs to be done.

Because stillness feels... unsafe.

Why?

Guilt – "If I'm not doing something for my family, I'm selfish."
Fear – "If I stop paying attention, everything will fall apart."
Habit – You've been in survival mode for so long that stillness feels foreign.

For many moms, rest doesn't feel restful — it feels uncomfortable. Your nervous system has learned that productivity equals safety. Doing equals control. Slowing down feels like losing your grip.

So you tell yourself you'll rest *later*.
After the kids are older.
After this busy season.
After things calm down.

But the seasons keep coming.

The first step isn't finding more time.
It's consciously *claiming* time for rest.

It's realizing you're allowed to stop — not because everything is finished, but because *you matter even when it's not*.

The Micro-Pause Principle

When I first started trying to slow down, I thought a "pause" had to be big to count.

A spa day.

A weekend away.

A long stretch of uninterrupted quiet.

Things I didn't have time for. Or money for. Or childcare for.

Then I realized something important:

A pause doesn't have to be long — it just has to be intentional.

That's when I started using what I call the **Micro-Pause Principle**:

Any moment you can step out of doing and into being counts as a pause — no matter how small.

Some of my first micro-pauses looked like this:

- Sitting in the driveway for two minutes before going inside after errands.

- Standing on the porch with my coffee while my son watched cartoons (don't come at me — Paw Patrol always saved the day).

- Turning off the radio and driving in silence instead of filling the space with noise.

These moments didn't change my schedule.
They didn't fix everything overnight.

But they changed *me*.

They reminded my body that it didn't have to stay braced all the time. That it was safe to soften — even briefly.

Why Small Pauses Matter So Much

Here's what most people don't understand: your nervous system doesn't need an hour to reset. It needs signals of safety.

Tiny pauses send that signal.

They tell your body:

"You're not in danger."

"You don't have to rush."

"You're allowed to exist without producing."

Over time, these moments add up. They create space between stimulus and response. They help you notice when you're holding your breath — before you're completely depleted.

Pausing isn't about stopping your life.
It's about staying present *inside* it.

How to Create Your First Pause

Let's make this practical and realistic.

Today, you're going to build a pause into your day on purpose — not when everything is done, but *because* you deserve it.

Choose the spot

Somewhere you can be alone for 1–5 minutes. Your

bedroom. The car. The bathroom. Wherever you can close the door — physically or mentally.

Pick the time
Attach it to something you already do every day. After school drop-off. After lunch. Before bed. No extra planning required.

Set the rule
During your pause: no phone, no chores, no planning. No "just real quick." You're not fixing anything. You're just noticing your breath, your body, and the fact that you exist.

Protect it
Treat this pause like an appointment. You wouldn't cancel a meeting with your boss for no reason — don't cancel this one with yourself.

What to Expect When You Start

The first few times, you might feel restless. You might think, *"This is pointless. I should be doing something."*

That's normal.

Your brain is used to constant stimulation. Your body is used to urgency. Stillness might feel uncomfortable — even threatening — at first.

But that discomfort isn't a sign you're doing it wrong.
It's a sign you're undoing years of conditioning.

Think of it like stretching a muscle you've been holding tight for years. At first, it feels awkward. Maybe even painful.

But over time, it becomes relief.

And eventually, pause stops feeling like a luxury…
and starts feeling like a necessity.

Action Step: Your 7-Day Pause Challenge

For the next seven days:

- Choose one pause each day.

- Keep it short (1–5 minutes).

- At the end of the week, jot down how you
  felt before and after each pause.

Journal/Reflection Prompt:

"If I made space to pause every day without
guilt, how might that change the way I show
up as a mom, partner, and human?"

Closing the Chapter

Giving yourself permission to pause isn't about "wasting time."
It's about reclaiming the space you need to breathe, think, and simply exist without constantly producing.

In the next chapter, we're going to take this even further by talking about *resetting your nervous system* — because once you've created the pause, you can use it to bring your whole body back into balance.

Chapter 5

Resetting Your Nervous System — Everyday techniques to calm your body.

Why Your Nervous System Matters More Than You Think

When you're a mom — especially one with a history of trauma — your nervous system often isn't reacting to what's happening *now*. It's reacting to everything it's learned to survive before.

Even on a regular Tuesday morning, your body might be operating like there's an emergency happening somewhere. Your heart races. Your muscles stay tight. Your patience runs thin. You feel on edge, even when nothing is technically wrong.

This isn't because you're dramatic, broken, or "too sensitive."

It's because your nervous system has learned to stay alert to keep you safe.

Think of your nervous system like a smoke alarm. When it's working properly, it alerts you to real danger. But when it becomes overly sensitive, it goes off when you're just making toast. Burnout, chronic stress, and unresolved trauma can crank that sensitivity way up.

Resetting your nervous system isn't about pretending stress doesn't exist. It's about teaching your body how to *return* to calm after stress passes — instead of staying stuck in survival mode all day, every day.

The Science-y Part (In Mom Language)

Your nervous system has two main operating modes:

Sympathetic Mode — *"Go, Go, Go"*
This is your body's emergency response system. It

increases heart rate, sharpens focus, and prepares you to act fast. It's helpful when your kid runs into the street or you need to slam on the brakes.

The problem? Many moms live here.

All. The. Time.

Parasympathetic Mode — *"Rest, Digest, Repair"*
This is where your body calms down. Digestion improves. Muscles relax. Hormones balance. Healing happens here — physically, emotionally, and mentally.

If you've been running on empty, chances are you've spent way too much time in sympathetic mode without enough parasympathetic breaks.

Here's the hopeful part:
Your nervous system is *trainable*.

With gentle, consistent practices, you can teach your body that it's safe to come back to calm — even in the middle of a busy life.

Signs Your Nervous System Needs a Reset

Sometimes we think stress has to look extreme to "count." In reality, nervous system overload often shows up quietly and persistently.

You might notice:

- Your thoughts won't slow down, even when you're exhausted

- Your body feels tense even when you're resting

- You startle easily or feel jumpy at small noises

- You feel emotionally numb or disconnected from yourself

- You get sick more often or deal with chronic aches and pains

These aren't personality flaws.
They're signs your system is overworked and under-supported.

Your body isn't betraying you — it's communicating.

Quick Reset Tools You Can Use Anywhere

These tools aren't about "fixing" yourself. They're about giving your body a clear message: *the threat has passed.*

1. The 4-4-6 Breath
Inhale through your nose for four counts

Hold for four counts

Exhale through your mouth for six counts

That longer exhale is key — it activates the calming branch of your nervous system. Repeat 3–5 times and notice how your body responds.

2. Grounding Through Your Senses

When your mind spirals, grounding brings you back to now. Slowly name:

- 5 things you see

- 4 things you feel

- 3 things you hear

- 2 things you smell

- 1 thing you taste

This pulls your brain out of "what if" mode and into the present moment.

3. Shake It Out

Animals instinctively shake after stress — and it works for humans too. Stand up and gently shake your arms, legs, shoulders, and torso for about 30 seconds. It releases stored tension and signals completion to your nervous system.

4. The Warm Hand Trick

Place one hand over your heart and the other on your belly. Feel your breath rise and fall. Gentle pressure and warmth stimulate the vagus nerve — a key player in calming your system.

5. "Sip" Water Mindfully

Slowly drink a glass of water, noticing the temperature and sensation with each sip. Hydration plus intentional slowing tells your body that it's safe enough to pause.

None of these require silence, privacy, or perfection. They work because your nervous system responds to *consistency*, not complexity.

The Bigger Picture Reset

Quick tools are powerful, but your nervous system also needs ongoing support. Think of this as creating a calmer baseline, not just crisis management.

Longer Term support looks like:

- **Daily movement** — not only workouts, just moving your body (walking absolutely counts)

- **Sleep** — as much as motherhood realistically allows

- **Nourishing food** — steady blood sugar helps stabilize mood and energy

- **Time outdoors** — nature naturally lowers stress hormones

- **Safe relationships** — trauma heals in connection, not isolation

- **Professional support** — therapy, coaching, or medical care when needed (asking for help is strength, not failure)

Resetting your nervous system isn't about doing everything perfectly. It's about giving your body enough safety cues that it doesn't have to stay on high alert all the time.

And when your body feels safer?
Everything else — patience, clarity, connection — becomes more accessible.

Action Step: Create Your Reset Menu

Make a list of five quick resets that work for you and keep it somewhere visible — on your fridge, inside your journal, or in your phone notes. That way, when stress spikes, you're not scrambling to remember what helps.

Journal/Reflection Prompt:

"When was the last time I felt truly calm in my body? What was I doing, and how can I add more of that into my week?"

Closing the Chapter

Your nervous system is not the enemy — it's your built-in alarm system. The goal isn't to silence it, but to help it recognize when you're safe.

In the next chapter, we'll talk about **how to set boundaries without guilt** so your nervous system isn't constantly pushed past its limits.

Chapter 6 –

Boundaries Without Guilt — Saying "no" without losing friends or family harmony.

Why Boundaries Feel So Hard for Moms

If you've ever said yes while every part of your body was screaming no, you're not alone.

For many moms — especially those with a trauma history — boundaries don't feel neutral. They feel loaded. Heavy. Dangerous, even. Saying no can trigger fears of being judged, rejected, or seen as selfish.

That's because, for a long time, many of us learned that being "good" meant being agreeable. Helpful. Easygoing. The mom who always shows up, always says yes, always stretches herself thinner for everyone else's comfort.

But here's the truth we were never taught:

A boundary is not a wall meant to keep people out.
It's a fence with a gate — and *you* control the latch.

Boundaries protect your time, energy, and mental
health so you can actually show up as the mom and
woman you want to be — not the version of you
that's exhausted, resentful, and running on fumes.

The Trauma Connection

When you've lived through situations where your
needs weren't respected, your nervous system
learns a powerful survival lesson: *keeping the peace
keeps you safe.*

That can show up as:

- Saying yes to avoid conflict

- Overextending yourself to "earn" love or approval

- Feeling responsible for other people's moods, reactions, or comfort

Your body may register boundary-setting as risky — even when you logically know it's healthy. That's not weakness. That's conditioning.

This is why Chapter 5 matters so much.

When your nervous system feels calmer and safer, setting boundaries becomes less terrifying. You're no longer trying to protect yourself *and* manage everyone else's emotions at the same time.

Boundaries get easier when your body believes you'll survive the discomfort.

The Three Types of Boundaries Every Mom Needs

Not all boundaries are confrontational or dramatic. Many are quiet, internal decisions that change how you show up.

Time Boundaries — *Protect Your Minutes and Hours*

Time is one of your most finite resources, yet it's often the one moms give away the fastest.

Example:

"I'm not available for calls after 8 PM."

This isn't rude. It's clear. And clarity prevents resentment.

Emotional Boundaries — *Protect Your Mental Space*

You are allowed to opt out of conversations, opinions, and emotional labor that drain you.

Example:

"I'm not in a place to discuss that right now."

You don't owe everyone access to your inner world.

Physical Boundaries — *Protect Your Body and Environment*
Your body belongs to you. Full stop.

Example:

"I don't want to be hugged without being asked."

Teaching boundaries here also teaches consent — to your kids and to others.

How to Set a Boundary Without Feeling Like the Villain

Boundary-setting doesn't have to be harsh. But it does have to be honest.

1. Get Clear on What You Need

You can't communicate a boundary you haven't defined for yourself.

Ask:

- What consistently drains me?

- What helps me feel regulated, calm, or supported?

Your needs matter — even if no one else has ever said that out loud.

2. Use Simple, Direct Language

You don't need a long explanation or a perfectly crafted speech.

Short and clear works best:
"That doesn't work for me."

Over-explaining often invites negotiation — and boundaries aren't debates.

3. Drop the Apology

"I'm sorry" is for when you've hurt someone — not for honoring your limits.

You can be kind *without* apologizing for existing.

4. Expect Discomfort

Some people will push back — especially if they've benefited from you having no boundaries.

Their reaction doesn't mean your boundary is wrong.
It means the dynamic is changing.

5. Follow Through

A boundary without follow-through is just a suggestion.

You're not *asking* people to respect your time, peace, and well-being.

You're *deciding* to protect it.

Scripts for Common Mom Situations

Sometimes guilt gets louder when we don't know what to say. These scripts give you a starting point — adjust them to sound like you.

When family drops by unannounced:
"I love seeing you, but I need a heads-up before visits. Let's set a time that works for both of us."

When someone comments on your parenting:
"I appreciate your concern, but I'm making choices that work for my family."

When you need time alone but feel guilty:
"I'm going to take an hour to myself so I can show up better for everyone later."

Notice none of these are aggressive.

They're calm. Clear. Grounded.

The Guilt Factor

Guilt is often the last thing to show up — and the hardest to sit with.

It shows up because:

- We were taught self-sacrifice equals good motherhood

- We fear losing approval, love, or connection

But here's the reframe that changes everything:

A boundary is an act of love.

You're modeling self-respect.
You're showing your kids what healthy relationships look like.

You're teaching them that caring for others doesn't require abandoning yourself.

That's not selfish.

That's leadership.

Action Step: Your First Low-Stakes Boundary

Start small. Choose one boundary you can set this week that feels uncomfortable but not terrifying. Write it down, say it out loud, and stick to it.

Journal Prompt:

"What's one area of my life where I feel resentful or drained? What boundary could help?"

Closing the Chapter

Boundaries are not about control — they're about clarity.

They let people know how to love and respect you in ways that work for you.

And when you model this for your kids, you give them permission to honor themselves too.

In the next chapter, we'll talk about **how to stop saying yes to everything** after years of self-abandonment, so your boundaries feel even more natural and unshakable.

Part 3:

Making Space in Your Life

Chapter 7

Declutter Your Calendar-

Stop Saying Yes to Everything

Why Your Calendar Is Making You Tired

If your calendar looks like a losing game of Tetris, it's not because you're bad at time management.

It's because you've been taught to measure your worth by how much you can juggle.

Many moms operate under an unspoken rule: *If I'm not busy, I'm not doing enough.*

So we fill the gaps. We stack commitments back-to-back. We treat empty space like a problem to solve instead of a gift to protect.

But a jam-packed calendar doesn't just keep you busy — it keeps you disconnected.

Disconnected from your body.
Disconnected from your needs.
Disconnected from the moments that actually make life feel meaningful.

When every hour is accounted for, there's no room for rest, spontaneity, or joy. There's only momentum — and momentum without intention leads straight to burnout.

The Hidden Cost of Overcommitting

Every yes comes with a cost.

When you say yes to everything, you're also saying no to something else:

- No to rest

- No to your own priorities

- No to showing up regulated, patient, and present

This is why you can reach the end of the week completely exhausted — yet unable to name a single moment that felt nourishing.

You weren't resting.
You weren't connecting.
You were just... managing.

Over time, this kind of living creates resentment — not necessarily toward others, but toward your own life. And that's a heavy thing to carry.

The Trauma Connection

For many moms, an overfilled calendar isn't just about poor boundaries — it's about survival.

If you grew up in an environment where love, safety, or approval were conditional, your nervous

system may still believe:
If I keep everyone happy, I'll be safe.

Busyness becomes a form of protection.
Availability becomes a coping strategy.
Overcommitting becomes proof that you're
"enough."

But here's the catch: when your schedule is
constantly packed, your body never gets the signal
that it's safe to slow down. There's no pause. No
recovery. No regulation.

Decluttering your calendar isn't just about time
management — it's about teaching your nervous
system that rest won't cost you connection or love.

Three Steps to Declutter Your Calendar

This isn't about blowing up your life or canceling everything. It's about choosing *intentionally* instead of automatically.

Step 1 — Audit Your Commitments
Take an honest look at your week.

Circle what's truly essential:

- Work

- Childcare

- Medical appointments

- Non-negotiable responsibilities

Now look at everything else and ask:
Is this aligned with my current season of life — or is it just habit, guilt, or obligation?

You're allowed to outgrow commitments.

Step 2 — Learn to Pause Before Saying Yes

One of the simplest but most powerful shifts you can make is this:

Instead of saying yes immediately, say:
"Let me check my schedule and get back to you."

This small pause interrupts guilt-driven responses and gives you space to feel into whether something is a genuine yes or a reflexive one.

If it's a true yes, you'll feel grounded.
If it's not, your body will tell you.

Step 3 — Protect White Space

White space isn't laziness.
It's breathing room.

Block off unscheduled time on your calendar and treat it like an unmovable appointment. No errands. No obligations. No productivity goals.

White space is where your nervous system recovers.
It's where creativity returns.
It's where you remember who you are outside of
responsibility.

Scripts to Say No Without Burning Bridges

Saying no doesn't have to be dramatic or harsh.
Clear and kind goes a long way.

- "Thanks for thinking of me, but I'm not able
  to commit right now."

- "That sounds great, but I need to protect
  some downtime this week."

- "I'm focusing on fewer commitments so I
  can be fully present for what matters most."

Notice: no over-explaining. No justifying your
worth. Just clarity.

Mini Boundaries for Your Calendar

Sometimes big changes feel overwhelming. These small boundaries can make a huge difference:

One Social Event Per Weekend
Avoid the Sunday-night exhaustion spiral by leaving space to reset.

Digital Detox Hours
Choose a cutoff time for emails and texts. Your brain needs an off switch.

Family Rest Day
One day with no plans and no pressure — not even "productive fun."

These aren't rules. They're supports.

The Freedom of a Decluttered Schedule

When you stop overfilling your calendar, you don't lose opportunities — you gain clarity.

You gain:

- More energy

- Better focus

- Space for the things you've been saying you want to do "someday"

And perhaps most importantly, you stop living on autopilot.

You start living intentionally — choosing a life that supports you instead of one you're constantly trying to survive.

Action Step: The Yes/No Filter

This week, before agreeing to anything, ask:

- Does this align with my values?

- Will this add joy or drain me?

- What will I have to give up to make space for this?

If it's not a clear Yes! Let's do this! — it's a No, thank you.

Journal/Reflection Prompt:

"If I could clear my schedule and rebuild it from scratch, what would I keep? What would I never add back?"

Closing the Chapter

Your time is your most valuable resource — and it's not refillable.
When you protect it, you protect your energy, your mental health, and the version of you your kids get to experience.

In the next chapter, we'll dive into **adding Micro-moments of Freedom**, so your life feels both calm and productive.

Chapter 8

Micro-Moments of Freedom: How to breathe even when you can't "get away."

Why Freedom Feels Out of Reach

When you picture "freedom," you might imagine a weeklong vacation, sleeping in without kids climbing on you, or a spa day with no responsibilities. And yes — that sounds absolutely lovely.

For many moms, freedom has become something distant and conditional — something that exists *after* the kids are older, *after* work slows down, or *after* you finally catch up.

But here's the truth most of us avoid: if we wait for big chunks of time to feel free, we'll spend years waiting.

Motherhood isn't built around long stretches of uninterrupted time. It's built around moments — short, messy, unpredictable ones. And when we dismiss those moments as "not enough," we unintentionally teach ourselves that our needs don't count unless they come in large, dramatic doses.

Freedom doesn't just live in vacations.
It lives in the tiny, intentional moments you claim for yourself — even in the middle of a busy, messy, motherhood-filled day.

The Myth of "When Things Calm Down"

You've probably said it before:
"When things calm down, I'll take time for myself."

This phrase sounds reasonable. Responsible, even. But it hides a dangerous assumption: that your nervous system can stay in survival mode indefinitely and be fine later.

The problem? Life rarely "calms down" on its own.

Motherhood has seasons, and even the quieter ones still require emotional labor, decision-making, and constant responsiveness. Waiting for calm means postponing relief — sometimes for years.

Micro-moments matter because they create *calm on purpose*. They tell your body it doesn't have to wait for permission to exhale.

What Are Micro-Moments?

Micro-moments are short, 1–5 minute pockets of intentional time where you:

- Breathe

- Reset your nervous system

- Reconnect with yourself

They are not self-care tasks to check off a list. They are moments of presence — moments where you stop bracing and start allowing.

They're not about escaping your life.
They're about reclaiming yourself *inside* of it.

Why They Work (The Nervous System Piece)

Your nervous system doesn't understand calendars or future promises. It only responds to what's happening *right now*.

When your days are filled with urgency, noise, and constant demands, your body assumes danger — even if nothing is technically "wrong."

Micro-moments interrupt that pattern.

Each pause sends a message:
I am safe in this moment.

Over time, these moments:

- Lower baseline stress

- Reduce irritability and snapping

- Increase patience with your kids and yourself

- Improve emotional regulation

- Restore a sense of control and choice

You're not fixing everything in five minutes. You're teaching your body that it doesn't have to stay on high alert all day.

10 Micro-Moments of Freedom for Moms

1. **Coffee Alone Before the Kids Wake Up –** Even three quiet sips before the day begins counts.

2. **Deep Breathing in the Car** – Park in the driveway for two extra minutes before going inside.

3. **A Song That's Yours** – Put on headphones and listen to your music while folding laundry.

4. **Step Outside** – Look at the sky, take three deep breaths, feel the air on your skin.

5. **The Locked-Bathroom Trick** – No shame in hiding for two minutes to regroup.

6. **Stretch Your Body** – Shoulder rolls, neck stretches or touching your toes.

7. **Light a Candle While You Work** – Let scent become a calming anchor.

8. **Take a Quiet Shower** – No bath. Just running water, warmth, and your own

thoughts. Trust me, a shower is much better for this kind of thing.

9. **One Page of a Book** – Doesn't have to be a whole chapter; one page still counts.

10. **Smile at Yourself in the Mirror** – Acknowledge you're doing the best you can.

When Micro-Moments Feel "Pointless"

Some days, a few deep breaths won't feel like enough. That doesn't mean they aren't working.

Trauma often convinces us that if something doesn't create instant relief, it isn't worth doing. But regulation is cumulative. It builds quietly, underneath the surface.

Think of micro-moments like deposits into an emotional savings account. One deposit doesn't change much — but over time, the balance grows.

How to Make Them Happen

Stack them onto what you already do.
Habit stacking makes micro-moments easier than trying to "find time." Take three deep breaths every time you wash your hands. Pause when you get into the car. Stretch while the coffee brews.

I do mine every time I take the dog out. Three deep breaths of fresh air — nothing fancy — but they anchor me back into my body.

Put them on your calendar.
Yes, even five minutes. Scheduling rest is not indulgent — it's protective.

Lower the bar.
If your brain says, *"This isn't enough,"* gently remind yourself: something is better than nothing.

Give yourself permission.
You don't need to earn rest, joy, or stillness by being productive first.

Reflection: Reclaiming Small Freedom

Ask yourself:

- Where in my day do I already pause — even briefly?

- What would it look like to make that pause intentional?

- What micro-moment feels most realistic for me right now?

Start with one. That's enough.

The Mindset Shift

When you start taking micro-moments, you send yourself a quiet but powerful message:

I matter too.

Not later. Not when things calm down. Not when you've done enough.

Now.

And that's the real detox — pulling your worth out of constant productivity and planting it in presence, self-trust, and moments of freedom that belong to you.

Action Step: Create a micro-moment
This week, choose **three** micro-moments from the list and commit to them daily.
Write them on a sticky note and put it somewhere you'll see them often.

Journal/Reflection Prompt:

"If I had five minutes just for me every day, what would I do with it?"

Closing the Chapter

Freedom isn't always a week away on a tropical beach.
Sometimes, it's in a quiet cup of coffee, a deep breath, or a favorite song played just for you.

In the next chapter, we'll explore how to **Delegate like a Boss**, even in the middle of chaos.

Chapter 9 –

Delegating Like a Boss: Getting help without feeling like a bad mom.

Why Delegating Feels So Hard for Moms

If you've ever thought:
"It's just easier if I do it myself."
or
"By the time I explain it, I could've already done it."

— you're not alone.

Many moms were raised to believe that asking for help means you're lazy, selfish, or failing at something you *should* be able to handle. Add a trauma history into the mix, and delegation can feel even harder. Trusting others, letting go of control, or relying on someone else might trigger fear, anxiety, or the belief that things will fall apart if you're not managing everything.

But here's the truth: **doing everything yourself isn't strength — it's survival mode.** And survival mode isn't where you're meant to live.

The Supermom Myth

We've been sold the idea that a "good mom" does it all — the cooking, cleaning, scheduling, emotional labor, school communication, and still somehow has energy left over.

Reality check: no one does it all alone.
They either have help, or they're quietly burning out.

Delegating isn't giving up control.
It's choosing sustainability over exhaustion.

Why Delegating Matters for Your Nervous System

When you're holding everything in your head —
appointments, meals, behavior management,
household needs — your nervous system never gets
to stand down. You're constantly scanning for what
needs to be done next.

Over time, this shows up as:

- Chronic fatigue

- Irritability and resentment

- Brain fog and forgetfulness

- Feeling disconnected from your own needs

Delegating creates space. And space tells your
nervous system: *We're supported. We don't have to
do this alone.*

Who You Can Delegate To

- **Your Partner** – This isn't "helping you"; it's shared responsibility. Delegating doesn't make you demanding — it makes you honest.

- **Your Kids** – Responsibility builds confidence. Even small tasks teach teamwork and independence.

- **Family & Friends** – Letting someone show up for you deepens connection — it doesn't weaken it.

- **Paid Help** – Think of it as outsourcing tasks, not your worth. You're buying back time and energy.

- **Tech & Tools** – Automation counts as delegation too.

How to Delegate Without Guilt

Decide What Actually Needs You
Some things require *you*. Many just need to be done.

Let Go of Perfection
Done imperfectly by someone else is better than done perfectly by an exhausted you at midnight.

Be Clear and Specific
Delegation works best when expectations are clear — no mind-reading required.

Release the "I Owe You" Mentality
Help doesn't have to be earned. You're allowed to receive support.

Remember: You're Modeling

When your kids see you delegate, they learn teamwork, communication, and that no one has to do life alone.

The "Delegate Like a Boss" Starter List

- Laundry folding

- Packing lunches

- Sweeping or vacuuming

- Scheduling appointments

- School paperwork

- Cooking one night a week

- Meal planning (even partially)

- Grocery pickup

- Yard work

- Pet care

Delegation isn't about doing less because you can't handle more.
It's about **doing what actually matters — and letting the rest go.**

Action Step: Delegate!

Choose **two tasks** you currently do that someone else *could* handle.
Delegate them this week — even if it feels uncomfortable.

Journal/Reflection Prompt:

"If I trusted others to support me, what's the first thing I'd hand off?"

Closing the Chapter

Delegating doesn't mean you're failing.
It means you're smart enough to protect your
energy so you can show up for what matters most.

Next up, we'll talk about **designing a daily, weekly
and seasonal ritual that works *with* your nervous
system instead of against it.**

Part 4:

Living with Space

Chapter 10 –

Rituals That Restore You: Daily, Weekly & Seasonal Grounding

Why Rituals Matter for Overloaded Moms

Rituals are more than routines.
They're intentional pauses that tell your nervous system, *"We're safe now. We can slow down."*

For overloaded moms, days can blur together into one long stretch of reacting — to kids, work, noise, mess, and needs. Rituals act like punctuation marks in your life. They create moments of meaning, transition, and grounding inside the chaos.

Unlike to-do lists, rituals don't exist to produce results.
They exist to **restore you**.

And when you're healing from trauma, restoration isn't optional — it's foundational.

The Trauma-Informed Twist

If you have a trauma history, the word *structure* can feel complicated. For some, it feels comforting. For others, it feels restrictive or even triggering.

That's why rituals are different from rigid schedules.

Rituals are **choice-based**, not demand-based. They're flexible, forgiving, and responsive to how you're actually feeling.

A ritual says: *"This is something I do to care for myself."*
A rigid routine says: *"This is something I have to do or I've failed."*

We're aiming for gentle rhythms — not perfection.

Daily Grounding Rituals

Think of these as micro-resets that bring your body out of autopilot and back into the present moment.

- **Morning Sunlight & Breath** – Step outside for two minutes. Inhale deeply. Let your eyes and nervous system register daylight.

- **The First Sip** – Before the day rushes in, notice the warmth, taste, and smell of your coffee or tea.

- **Five-Minute Body Scan** – Release tension from your jaw, shoulders, and belly. These are common stress storage zones.

- **Evening Transition** – Dim the lights, light a candle, or play soft music to signal to your body that the day is ending.

Trauma-informed reminder: Choose rituals that feel safe and soothing **in your body**, not ones that look good on paper.

Weekly Grounding Rituals

Weekly rituals help you discharge the stress that builds up over time.

- **Sunday (or Any-Day) Check-In** – Look at the week ahead and choose your top three priorities — not everything.

- **Nature Reset** – A walk, park visit or simply standing outside and breathing fresh air.

- **Digital Detox Hour** – Put your phone in another room and give your brain a break from constant input.

- **Family Connection Time** – No multitasking. Just presence.

Trauma-informed tip: Keep the day consistent but allow the time to stay flexible so the ritual doesn't become another obligation.

Seasonal Grounding Rituals

Your body changes with the seasons — your self-care should too.

- **Spring** – Declutter one small space. Open windows. Invite light and movement.

- **Summer** – Claim early morning outdoor time before the heat and noise take over.

- **Fall** – Slow your pace intentionally. Warm drinks, cozy layers, gentler evenings.

- **Winter** – Rest more. Move gently. Let yourself soften. Winter was designed for rest — resisting that only creates burnout.

Seasonal rituals remind you that slowing down, shifting focus, and needing different things at different times is not failure — it's wisdom.

Building Your Ritual Rhythm

- **Start Small** – One daily ritual, one weekly, one seasonal.

- **Layer Gently** – Add more only when it feels supportive, not forced.
  Link to Existing Habits – Stack rituals onto things you already do.

- **Honor Resistance** – If you skip a ritual, don't shame yourself. Just begin again.

Rituals aren't about doing more.
They're about **coming home to yourself — again and again — no matter how full life gets.**

Action Step: Create a Ritual

Write down *one* ritual you'll start today, one you'll start this week, and one you'll adopt for the current season.

Journal/Reflection Prompt:

"What simple action instantly makes me feel more grounded — and how can I do it more often?"

Closing the Chapter

Rituals aren't about being perfect. They're about giving your nervous system repeated evidence that you're safe, cared for, and allowed to slow down.

The more you practice, the more these pauses become a natural part of your life — not just survival mode, but moments of genuine restoration.

Chapter 11 –

Choosing What Actually Matters: Aligning Your Life with Your Values

---

When "Supermom" Becomes a Distraction

Most moms I work with are drowning in tasks that look important but don't actually line up with what matters most to them. We say yes to bake sales, overcommit to work projects, join group chats we secretly hate — all while saying no to rest, connection, and joy.

Why?
Because busyness feels safer than stillness.

Stillness leaves room for our feelings, fears, and unmet needs to surface. It can be uncomfortable to sit with the fact that we're tired, resentful, or craving more than what our current routines provide. So we fill our days with "busy work" to avoid the vulnerability of checking in with ourselves.

But here's the truth: when your daily life matches your **real values** — not what you think you *should* value — you create space for genuine peace, purpose, and presence. Life stops feeling like a series of obligations and starts feeling intentional.

The Trauma-Informed Twist

If you've experienced trauma, your internal compass may have been hijacked by survival mode. You might find yourself:

- Saying yes to avoid conflict or rejection.

- Prioritizing others' needs to feel safe or loved.

- Feeling guilty for wanting anything that benefits you.

Aligning with your values isn't selfish — it's reclaiming your life. It's teaching your nervous system that your needs matter too. And when you start living according to your values, even small decisions feel lighter, freer, and more grounded.

Step 1: Define Your True Values

Grab a journal and write down:

- What lights me up?

- What makes me feel calm and safe?

- What do I want my kids to remember about our life together?

Examples of core values for moms:

- Family connection

- Health & vitality

- Creativity

- Spiritual growth

- Simplicity & ease

Notice the difference between what society tells you to value and what **truly resonates** with your heart. This is your north star — your map out of autopilot living.

Step 2: Identify the "Value Leaks"

A value leak happens when your time, energy, or money goes to something that doesn't align with your priorities.

Examples:

- Saying yes to events you dread.

- Scrolling social media when rest or reflection is what you really need.

- Overcommitting at work to avoid feeling "lazy."

- Attending meetings or volunteering out of obligation rather than desire.

Recognizing leaks is freeing — it's not about judging yourself, it's about noticing where energy is escaping without intention.

Step 3: Choose Your Filter

Before committing to anything, ask yourself:

- Does this align with at least one of my top three values?

- If I say yes, what am I saying no to?

- Will this matter a year from now?

If the answer is "no" or you feel that pit in your stomach, **let it go**. Practicing this filter builds confidence and trust in your own decision-making.

Step 4: Align Your Calendar

Your calendar is a mirror of your priorities. If it's crammed with obligations you resent, autopilot is running the show — not your values.

- Block time for your values first (family, rest, creative time, health).

- Let the rest of your commitments fill in after.

- Treat value-based commitments as non-negotiable, like appointments with yourself.

Trauma-informed tip: When you start saying "no" to things that drain you, guilt will show up. That's normal. It's not a sign you're doing it wrong — it's a sign you're **doing it differently**.

Reflection Exercise: Your Values in Action

1. Look at your upcoming week. Circle any activities that don't align with your values.

2. Choose one thing you can let go of or delegate.

3. Replace it with a value-aligned activity — even if it's just 15 minutes of reading, walking, or breathing.

Small shifts like these add up, building a life that feels **intentional, calm, and aligned** rather than frenzied, reactive, and exhausting.

Action Step: Identify Your Values

Write down your **top three values**.
 For the next week, run every new request through your values filter before saying yes.

Journal/Reflection Prompt:

"If I could design my days to match my values perfectly, what would they look like?"

Closing the Chapter

When you choose what actually matters and live in alignment with your values, you're no longer just surviving motherhood — you're leading your life with intention.
 You become the kind of mom who models for her

kids that *their* lives can be shaped around what matters most to them too.

Chapter 12 –

Thriving Beyond Survival Mode: Building a Future You Actually Want to Live In

---

The Shift from "Making It Through" to "Loving Your Life"

For so long, survival mode has been your default. You've been juggling diapers, deadlines, dinner, and deep emotional exhaustion. You've gotten really good at pushing through.

But here's the truth no one tells you:
You can't live in survival mode forever without losing parts of yourself along the way.

Thriving isn't just having more energy — it's having more life.
It's waking up not just to check off a to do list, but

to live in a way that feels meaningful, connected, and yours.

Thriving means feeling the **small sparks of joy in everyday life** and building a life that aligns with your values and priorities — even amidst the chaos of motherhood.

Why Survival Mode Feels "Safer" Than Thriving

If you've experienced trauma, survival mode may feel familiar. It's predictable. It keeps your nervous system on high alert, which — ironically — can feel safer than the vulnerability of joy.

Thriving requires you to:

- Believe good things are possible for you.

- Risk disappointment by dreaming bigger.

- Allow rest without guilt.

At first, it can feel scary. Your body and brain have learned to expect danger, discomfort, or overwork. Thriving feels unfamiliar — and that's okay. It's a skill you can cultivate, one small choice at a time.

Step 1: Decide What Thriving Means for You

Thriving is not a one-size-fits-all Pinterest board. It's deeply personal.

Ask yourself:

- What would my ideal day look like?

- What relationships would I nurture?

- How would I take care of my mind, body, and spirit?

- What would I stop tolerating?

Write down even the "impossible" dreams. Don't self-edit. Let your imagination stretch. Your nervous system needs to **experience possibility** before it can believe joy is safe.

Step 2: Build from Your Values Up

(See Chapter 11 — your values are the foundation.)

Once you know your top values, ask:

- How can I weave them into my daily life right now?

- What bigger changes will I need to make over time?

Values are your compass — they make decisions simpler and reduce stress by cutting out obligations that don't align with your life vision.

Step 3: Dream Without the "Yeah, But"

When you picture your future, notice if you shut it down with thoughts like:

- "Yeah, but I don't have the time/money/support."

- "Yeah, but my kids need me too much."

For now, don't solve those barriers — just **dream anyway**. Imagine the life you want, without limitation. Dreaming in this safe space tells your nervous system: **it's okay to want joy, and it's okay to experience it.**

Step 4: Start Thriving in Microdoses

You don't have to overhaul your life in a week. Thriving starts with tiny, repeatable choices that signal to your body, *We're safe now.*

Examples:

- Drinking your coffee outside instead of over the sink.

- Listening to music you love while cooking.

- Taking five minutes to breathe before responding to a stressful text.

- Closing your laptop for 10 minutes to stretch or step outside.

These micro-moments create momentum. Over time, they **rewrite your nervous system's default** from survival to safety, rest, and pleasure.

Step 5: Make Thriving Your New Normal

- Schedule joy, not just tasks. Even 15 minutes counts.

- Surround yourself with people who support your growth and celebrate your wins.

- Keep a "thriving journal" where you jot down moments you felt alive, grateful, or proud.

Over time, thriving stops feeling like a vacation you have to earn — and starts feeling like home.

Reflection Exercise: Thriving Checklist

1. Write down three micro-moments you can add to your day this week that would feel nourishing.

2. Identify one boundary you can set that protects space for joy.

3. Visualize your ideal day this weekend. What's one small step you can take to move toward it?

Trauma-Informed Tip: Stay with Joy

It's common to feel an urge to "sabotage" thriving moments — rushing through them, finding fault, or distracting yourself. This is your nervous system testing the **safety of joy**.

Stay with it. Practice small, safe moments of joy daily. Over time, they become familiar, your nervous system relaxes and **thriving stops feeling risky — it starts feeling natural.**

You've spent years surviving. Now it's time to thrive. Not someday, not when everything is perfect, but **right here, right now**, in small, deliberate, life-affirming choices.

Action Step: Write Your Vision Story

Write a one-page "vision story" of your life one year from now, describing it in the present tense as if it's already your reality. Read it every morning for the next 30 days.

Journal/Reflection Prompt:

"If my survival mode self could see my thriving self, what would she thank me for?"

Closing the Book, Opening Your Future

You've detoxed from the myths and pressures of Supermom culture.
You've reset your nervous system, reclaimed your time, and reconnected to your values.
Now, you get to decide what's next.

139

Thriving isn't a destination — it's a way of showing up for your own life, every single day.

It's giving yourself permission to live a future you don't just endure, but *adore*.

Conclusion –

This Is Where Things Change

If you're still holding this book in your hands, I
want you to pause for a second.
Not to rush into fixing anything.
Not to add another "should" to your list.

Just to notice this: **you showed up for yourself.**

In a culture that praises exhaustion and glorifies
doing it all, choosing to slow down, reflect, and care
for your inner world is a radical act. You didn't pick
this book because you're failing — you picked it
because something inside you knew there had to be
another way to live.

Over these chapters, you've peeled back layers you
might not have had words for before. You've
named the invisible load. You've challenged the
Supermom myth. You've learned how your nervous
system has been trying to protect you — even when

it felt like it was working against you. You've practiced pausing, setting boundaries, delegating, creating rituals, and aligning your life with what actually matters.

None of this was about becoming a "better" mom. It was about becoming a **more supported, regulated, present, and human one.**

You don't need to overhaul your life overnight. You don't need to do all the tools perfectly. And you definitely don't need to earn rest, peace, or joy by burning yourself out first.

What you *do* need is consistency, compassion, and a way to turn these insights into something you can actually live — on your busiest days, not just your best ones.

That's where the **Supermom Detox Plan** comes in.

The plan ahead isn't about restriction or rigid rules. It's about gently clearing out what's draining you and intentionally making space for what restores you. Think of it as a reset — not of who you are, but of how you care for yourself while you care for everyone else.

Some days you'll nail it. Some days you'll forget every tool you've learned and snap at someone over spilled blueberries. Both are part of the process. Growth isn't linear, and healing certainly isn't either.

So take a deep breath.
Loosen the cape.
You don't have to survive your way through life anymore.

You're allowed to rest.
You're allowed to ask for help.
You're allowed to build a life that feels good to live in.

Let's detox — together.

You Don't Have to Do This Alone

If this book resonated with you, chances are you've been carrying more than anyone realizes — maybe even more than *you* realized before now.

Reading, reflecting, and practicing these tools is powerful.
And sometimes, having support while you do it is what makes the biggest difference.

This is where we can work together.

Support for Moms Healing from Survival Mode

I work with mothers who are:

- Emotionally exhausted but still showing up for everyone else

- Healing from trauma, chronic stress, or burnout

- Trying to break cycles without breaking themselves

- Ready to feel more regulated, present, and grounded in daily life

My approach is trauma-informed, nervous-system-aware, and deeply human. There's no fixing, no shaming, and no pressure to be "better" — just support that meets you where you are.

Ways to Work Together

Depending on where you're at, support might look like:

- 1:1 support focused on nervous system regulation, boundaries, and sustainable self-care

- Group support with other moms who get it

- Workshops and guided programs designed to help you move from survival to thriving

All of my work is built around one core belief: You deserve support while you heal — not after.

Ready When You Are

There's no rush. No deadline. No "right" pace. If and when you're ready to take the next step, I'd love to support you.

You can learn more, explore current offerings, or simply connect at:

www.evergreenpathwaysllc.com
jessica@evergreenpathwaysllc.com
www.facebook.com/everygreenpathwayswellness
www.instagram.com/jessica.evergreenpathways

Whether this is the end of your journey with this book or the beginning of deeper support, I'm honored to have walked alongside you.

You don't have to do this alone anymore.

— *Jessica Belch*
Evergreen Pathways

The Supermom Detox Plan

A Practical Roadmap to Go from Surviving to Thriving

You've read the stories. You've done the reflections.

Now, let's put it all into motion.

This is your **step-by-step guide** to actually living the change you've been craving.

This isn't about hustling harder or trying to "fix" yourself — you were never broken.

It's about **intentionally building a life that feels like it fits** you, not the one the world told you to wear.

Phase 1 – The Reset *(Weeks 1–3)*

Goal: Calm your nervous system and get out of constant fight-or-flight mode.

1. **Create your daily nervous system ritual** (Chapter 1)

   o Example: Five deep breaths before getting out of bed, coffee on the porch, gentle stretching.

2. **Detox your mom-myths** (Chapter 2)

   o Write down every "good mom should..." belief you've carried and cross out the ones that aren't yours.

3. **Conduct an Energy Tank Audit** (Chapter 3)

   ○ Rate your physical energy, emotional energy and mental clarity from 1-10. Mark your calendar every 30 days recommit the this audit.

4. **Start practicing nervous system safety in micro-moments** (Chapter 4)

   ○ Ground yourself when you feel triggered — use touch, movement, or breath.

Phase 2 – The Reclaim *(Weeks 5–8)*

Goal: Take back your time, space, and energy.

1. **Identify your long-term support plan**
    (Chapter 5)

    - Identify what tools you can use,
      long-term, to help support your
      emotional and mental well-being.
      This can be consistent time outdoors,
      scheduled family time each week or
      hiring professional help (counselor,
      coach etc.)

2. **Learn to say no without guilt** (Chapter 6)

    - Start small — decline one thing this
      week that doesn't align with your
      values.

3. **Delegate like a boss** (Chapter 9)

- ○ Hand off one recurring task at home or work, even if you have to teach someone first.

Phase 3 – The Align *(Weeks 9–12)*

Goal: Live in line with what actually matters to you.

1. **Clarify your top 5 values** (Chapter 11)

   - ○ Use them as a decision filter: *If it doesn't match my values, it's a no.*

2. **Build restoring rituals** (Chapter 10)

   - ○ Daily: something small (like tea before bed).

- Weekly: something grounding (like Sunday walks).

- Seasonal: something soul-filling (like a family day trip).

3. **Protect your energy like currency**

   - You can only do so much. Before committing to anything this week, take a pause and reflect on your current commitments and if it will bring you joy or drain your soul. Decide if you can REALLY afford to say yes…

Phase 4 – The Thrive *(Ongoing)*

Goal: Build a future you actually want to live in.

1. **Dream bigger than survival** (Chapter 12)

   ○ Write your 1-year vision and read it daily. Write it in present tense, like you are already living that life, trust me, this helps.

2. **Add in more joy, not more tasks**

   ○ Schedule fun and rest like they're doctor's appointments.

3. **Stay in community**

   ○ Keep connecting with people who support your healing and growth.

This can be in the community, your family or virtual support groups and connections.

Quick-Glance Detox Checklist

- ☐ Daily nervous system ritual

- ☐ One outdated "good mom" rule eliminated

- ☐ Weekly no-guilt "no"

- ☐ One delegated task

- ☐ Values list posted somewhere visible

- ☐ Daily joy microdose

- ☐ 1-year vision written and reviewed

Remember:

Healing is not linear. You will have days where you
slip into survival mode again — that's okay.
The goal isn't to be perfect.
The goal is to *notice sooner*, recover faster, and
keep moving toward the life you're building.

You are not here to be a martyr to motherhood.
You're here to be a whole, healthy, deeply alive
woman — who also happens to be a mom.

That's the real ***Supermom Detox***.

About the Author

Jessica Belch

Jessica is a mental health professional, writer, and mother who understands firsthand how quietly overwhelming motherhood can become. She is married, raising two boys, and lives with her family in a rural Maine town, where life is both deeply meaningful and relentlessly demanding.

For a long time, Jessica embraced the "SuperMom" label, until she realized it was pulling her into unsustainable patterns, chronic exhaustion, and burnout. Finding her way out of that cycle changed everything. Now, with a background in clinical rehabilitation counseling and a passion for compassionate, realistic support, she helps other moms release the mental load, question impossible expectations, and reconnect with themselves without guilt or perfection.

Through her writing, community spaces, and future private practice, Jessica offers a steady, hopeful path forward for overwhelmed moms who are ready for relief, not more pressure.

www.ingramcontent.com/pod-product-compliance
Lightning Source LLC
LaVergne TN
LVHW051411080426
835508LV00022B/3038